John Calvin

What is the truth?

The true story of John Calvin and the Reformation

Catherine Mackenzie
Illustrated by Rita Ammassari

John Calvin lived in the city of Noyon in the country of France over 500 years ago. He had a father and several brothers, but his mother had died when he was just a young boy.

John was clever and loved to read. He longed to go to school. He knew that if he got a good education it would mean great things for his life. His father encouraged him to do his best and work hard.

John was clever and loved to read.

When John went to school he got a special hair cut called a tonsure. It was strange at first but all the other boys looked the same. They wore the same clothes too.

John learned his lessons well. His best friends were both from rich families and they let John study at their homes. So it wasn't long before John was doing very well at school. His father was delighted.

When John went to school he got a special hair cut.

On his way to school, John could hear bells ringing. The cathedral was very near his home. When he peered up into the sky he could see large, strong walls surrounding all the streets and buildings.

The cathedral bells were there to tell people to come and worship God. The walls of the city were there to protect the people from enemy attack.

John could hear bells ringing.

But the real danger was that John didn't know the truth about God. John's priest told him that you could get to heaven by being good or by paying money to the church. This wasn't true. Nobody is good enough to get into heaven. Nobody can buy a place there.

Jesus Christ is the only way to heaven. He is the only one good enough to pay the price that is needed. When Jesus died on the cross he did all that is required to forgive sinners and obtain everlasting life for them. John, however, didn't know about that.

John didn't know the truth about God.

One day, John saddled his horse and set off for university. It was sad that even though he was very clever, he didn't know what to do about the wrong things he had done. He didn't know what to do about his sins.

However, when he arrived at Paris, John read what Martin Luther had written. John then realised that to have peace with God you had to trust in God's Son – Jesus. God the Father had sent his one and only Son to save sinners. Those sinners who believed in Jesus Christ, God's Son, would be forgiven for their sins and have everlasting life.

John read what Martin Luther had written.

John had always been taught that you had to pray to Mary and the saints for forgiveness. But this wasn't true. When he met other people who had been forgiven, John realised that he could pray to God directly. It was an exciting time for John as he discovered all these truths.

However, many Reformers like John were being thrown in prison, so it was a dangerous time too.

John realised that he could pray to God directly.

John Calvin also started to read the Bible. He had seen Bibles before in Cathedrals, but they were read by priests usually and not by ordinary people. That was because the Bible was written in a language that very few people understood. The priests didn't want people reading it for themselves.

When John read the Bible for himself he began to realise what an important book it was.

John Calvin also started to read the Bible.

It didn't take long for John to realise that the priests had been lying to him. He trusted in Jesus Christ to save him from his sins and started to tell others the truth that they hadn't heard.

John travelled far and wide. Many people didn't like what he said. However, what John was saying was true. It was the Church that had been wrong.

John travelled far and wide.

John had to run away to another country. His enemies wanted to put him in prison. Eventually, he arrived in Geneva where he hoped to be able to teach the truth in safety. Unfortunately, John had enemies there too. Thankfully, there was one person in Geneva who loved him and looked after him – his wife, Idellete. When Idellete's first husband died she was left on her own with her two children. Eventually, Idellete and John Calvin became husband and wife. John was thankful to God for his new family.

Many other people who lived in Geneva at that time knew that John Calvin was preaching the truth, so they listened eagerly to all that he had to say.

John had to run away to another country.

God helped John Calvin to teach the truth. He was one of the men who started what we now call the Reformation. Men and women who listened to John's preaching decided that they had to tell others, too.

John helped them to go to other countries to teach the truth about God. Some even travelled thousands of miles across oceans. A new church had begun – a reformed church.

God helped John Calvin to teach the truth.

John Calvin died in Geneva, nobody knows for sure where he is buried. However, people today remember John Calvin because of the truth that he taught. John taught the truth so that we can learn it, believe it and live by it.

We must thank God for the men and women of the Reformation who believed in Him and spread His truth across the world.

People today remember John Calvin because of the truth that he taught.

This book is written for my parents,
William and Carine Mackenzie,
who taught me the truth of God's Word.

Teach them to your children, talking about them when you sit at home and when you walk along the road, when you lie down and when you get up.
Deuteronomy 11:19

ISBN: 978-1-84550-560-8
Reprinted 2013, 2016, 2022 and 2026

Published by Christian Focus Publications,
Geanies House, Fearn, Tain, Ross-shire, IV20 1TW, Scotland, U.K.
www.christianfocus.com

Cover design by Daniel van Straaten
Printed by Imprint, India